Sea Faeries

JILLIAN SAWYER

Photography
Chris Garnett

Published by
The Original Redback Press

For my sister Gaye, and brothers Lee and Neil.
'We each have our own memories to treasure and share'.
and for Dad,
'Who left us with cherished memories of golden days'.

Mum, Granite Island, South Australia, 1939

Published by The Original Redback Press
PO Box 891 Subiaco Western Australia 6904
February 1998
Printed by Prime Packaging Industries Pte Ltd, Singapore

FOREWORD

I haven't seen the ocean in ages now, but how easily I call it to mind.

Wild howling nights where our father would bundle us out of bed into the car to see the power and majesty of the sea thundering over the roadways, mountainous spray reaching high and the roadway crumbling under its might.

Night time crabbing on the jetty, cold nights when my bones ached with growing pains - but what fun hauling up the nets filled with crabs, or just weed and myriad strange little sea creatures

Watching the phosphorous play across the tops of the waves or in the wake of the boats.

Standing on the shore, watching him wade waist to neck deep to circle in the nets - sometimes just hearing the voices because it was so dark and wondering how they had the nerve - there were sharks in those South Australian waters!

Dad pointing and saying "See the white horses dancing in the rolling waves" and I swear I'd see them and I see them still.

Memories of a childhood holiday, lifting wads of seaweed and finding strips of green glassy beads that burst when you squeezed them and bright green sea lettuce that had been washed in.

Granite Island, where we stuck our heads through holes weathered by sea, as our mothers and theirs, had done before us.

The wind sending the sand stinging on our legs.

Day visits to Marine Rocks and exploring the rock pools there - lifting shells and finding tiny octopi inside, or hermit crabs, or just catching the little rock crabs whose claws were too small to do much harm.

Just the days at the local beach where I tried for hours in vain to catch just one of the scores of tiny fish swarming in the shallows - or the magnificent sandcastles of childhood, built on the tide line with ramparts and moats and watching them wash away.

Digging in the sand with our toes for cockles and just picking up shells - tiny iridescent ones or glorious, fragile, bright yellow and pink fan shells, dyed that colour by the sun. The competitions we had to see who could find the smallest - the excitement of the find and the disappointment when our find proved to be only half a shell in the sand, the rest crushed, to become part of that same sand.

The curling white caps, the glassy expanses, jellyfish (little banana shaped creatures that we used to skip across the surface of the sea - poor things). A shell, the foamy incursions onto the sand - I'd see things there and picture them so.

These recalled sensations and memories bless my mind and help bring my fantasized mermaids to vivid life.

My Faeries of the Sea, bewitching and alluring, please share them with me.

Jillian Sawyer
Firebird Leadlights
P.O. Box 522
Cannington
Western Australia 6107
Phone or fax 61 8 9362 6259
Email firebird@inf.net.au

STREAM
THE LURE OF THE SEA

Oh, how I love the sea!
Elemental your force
Relentless your course
Ebb and flow over me.

SPRAY
THE DANCE OF THE GOLDEN SEA FANS

*Rapt, she is caught by the rhythms of
the seas and sways seductively to its music,
her golden sea fans put to magnificent use.*

GLASS CHOICE:
Hair - bronze
Body - amber machined antique
Tail - patterned iridised antique
Fins - amber/clear streaky

TECHNICAL DETAILS

Spikes on fins are tinned copperwire overlaid for the full length of the seams for a raised effect. Hanging loop into hair seam, edge beading for strength and features painted.

SPRAY
THE DANCE OF THE GOLDEN SEA FANS

GLASS CHOICE:
Hair - red baroque
Body - red/clear flashed bariole
Tail - orangy red seashell
Fins - red/amber seedy
Sea fans - amber seedy

TECHNICAL DETAILS

Twisted strands of tinned copperwire are overlaid on the two main cuts of each fan, fanning out at the ends, then more added and attached at strategic places (so there is no movement). See photograph. Hanging loop positioned at hair and sea fan join, edge beading for finish and features painted with black enamel.

7

RIPPLE
LOVE THOUGHTS

I tend my hair as I think of you
for I know how you love it so.
The shining long tresses slip like silk through my fingers
And I ache for your soft sweet kisses

DAMSIN
BOBBING ALONG

I'm going for a float on my paper nautilus boat.
Bobbing happily atop the waves and singing merrily,
Perched upon my dainty shell, cradled by the sea.

RIPPLE
LOVE THOUGHTS

GLASS CHOICE:
Hair - clear iridised ripple
Body - flesh coloured spectrum
Tail - blue seashell
Fins - blue/green/purple streaky

TECHNICAL DETAILS

Hanging loop positioned at top hair join.
Edge beading for strength and finish.
Features painted.

DAMSIN
BOBBING ALONG

GLASS CHOICE:
Hair - amber/clear streaky
Body - pale violet mouthblown antique
Tail - grape waterglass
Fins - purple/clear streaky
Shell - milky white ripple
Seaweed - green/brown/clear streaky

TECHNICAL DETAILS

Hanging loop at hair join, edge beading for professional finish and features painted.

SWIRL AND EDDY
PENGUIN FUN

Oh, what a happy penguin you are!
Such joy you bring to me.
You race back and forth
Like a lovesick dork
And make me laugh with glee!

VIVIENNE AND "KILLER"
WALKING THE DOG

*Lets get decked out in our finery and go for a lovely walk
We'll sashay down to the grand parade and make them sit up and talk!
Everyone there will gasp and point as you pirouette and I wiggle my derriere
We'll knock 'em dead with our stunning grace and our daring savoir - faire.*

SWIRL AND EDDY
PENGUIN FUN

GLASS CHOICE:
Mermaid
Hair - amber
Body - gold pink mouthblown antique
Tail - teal waterglass
Fins - teal baroque

Water Stream
Alt deutsch

Penguin
Upperbody - black
Underbody - white
Beak - bone opal

TECHNICAL DETAILS

Hair piece can be tinned metal shell soldered to hair, a cut glass shell or simply continue hair line as in large panel on page 32. Side clips for hair piece are crab slashers in jewellery finding soldered to hair line.

Penguin's eye is solder blob. Position hanging loop behind shell in hair. Edge beading for professional finish. Features painted in black enamel.

VIVIENNE AND "KILLER"
WALKING THE DOG

GLASS CHOICE:
Mermaid
Body - gold pink mouthblown antique
Tail - turquoise
Fins - blue/green streaky
Hair - amber/clear streaky

Sea Horse
Head - brown ripple
Back - brown ripple
Tail - brown ripple
Belly - rose brown
Fin - cinnamon baroque

Water Stream
Clear waterglass

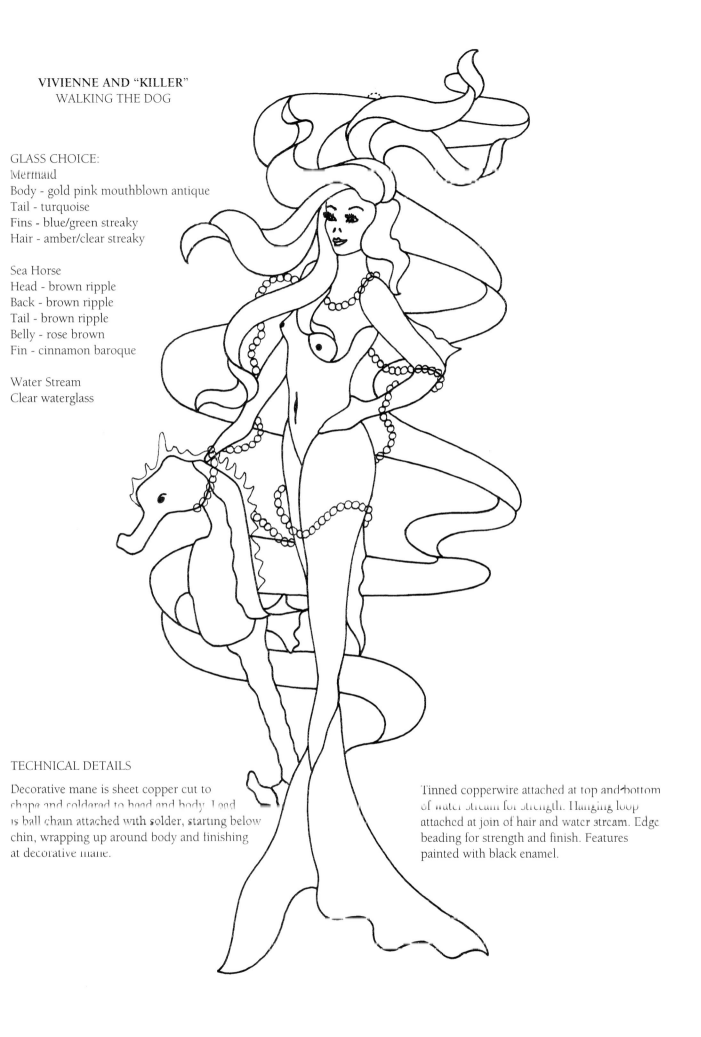

TECHNICAL DETAILS

Decorative mane is sheet copper cut to shape and soldered to head and body. Lead is ball chain attached with solder, starting below chin, wrapping up around body and finishing at decorative mane.

Tinned copperwire attached at top and bottom of water stream for strength. Hanging loop attached at join of hair and water stream. Edge beading for strength and finish. Features painted with black enamel.

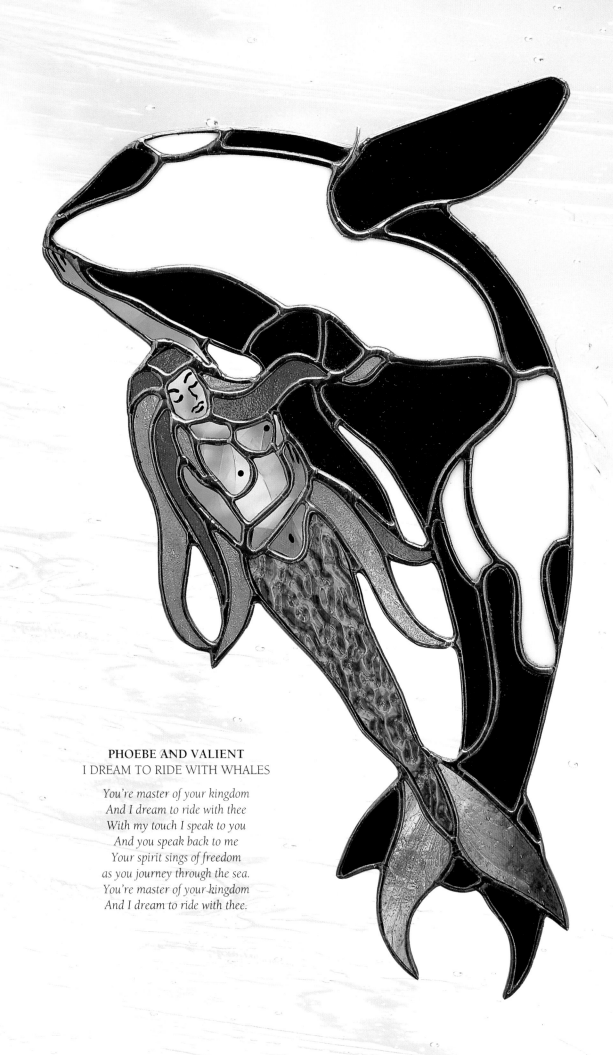

PHOEBE AND VALIENT
I DREAM TO RIDE WITH WHALES

You're master of your kingdom
And I dream to ride with thee
With my touch I speak to you
And you speak back to me
Your spirit sings of freedom
as you journey through the sea.
You're master of your kingdom
And I dream to ride with thee.

CRYSTAL AND SNOWFLAKE
THE LONG WAIT

Don't worry little ice pup -
Wait and you will see
Mummy is coming back to you -
Until then, you're safe with me.

PHOEBE AND VALIENT
I DREAM TO RIDE WITH WHALES

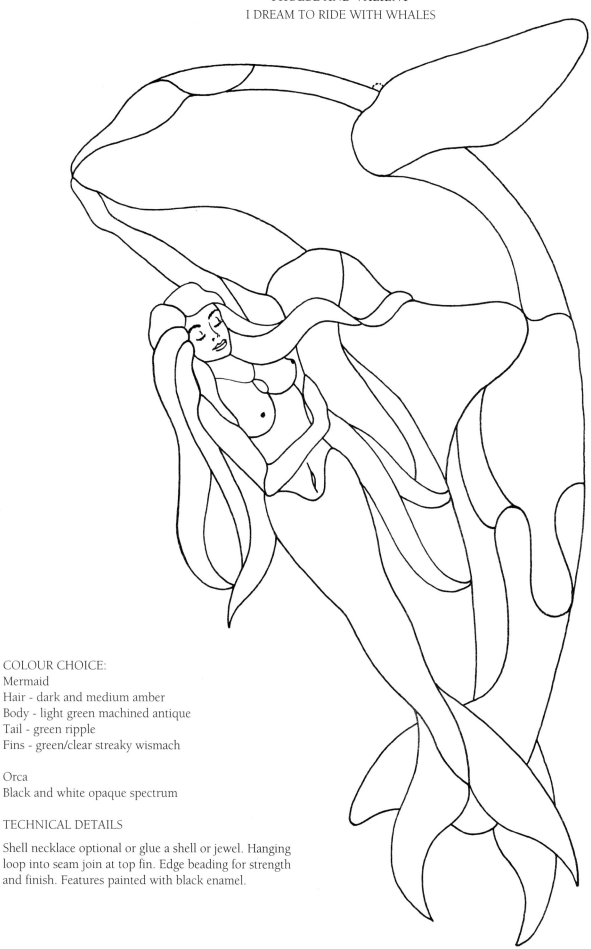

COLOUR CHOICE:

Mermaid

Hair - dark and medium amber

Body - light green machined antique

Tail - green ripple

Fins - green/clear streaky wismach

Orca

Black and white opaque spectrum

TECHNICAL DETAILS

Shell necklace optional or glue a shell or jewel. Hanging loop into seam join at top fin. Edge beading for strength and finish. Features painted with black enamel.

COLOUR CHOICE:
Mermaid
Hair - clear iridised ripple
Body - turquoise mouthblown antique
Tail - teal ripple
Fins - teal baroque

Baby Harp Seal
Body - cream opaque
Muzzle - lighter cream opaque
Eyes - black
Nose - black

Ice
Teal/white opaque
Teal/white streaky

TECHNICAL DETAILS

Whiskers tinned copperwire attached to solder seams on muzzle and head, with top whisker hiding cut line. Hanging loop soldered into hair line. Edge beading for strength and neat finish. Features painted with black enamel.

CILLA AND CECIL
MY PROTECTOR

We make a great team, you and I Cess,
I'd never betray you, I'd never confess.
They'll never know, they think you're so tough
You're just a big softy and it's all a huge bluff!

SERENDIPITY
CORAL CONTEMPLATION

*As I sit at my coral table top in quiet contemplation,
I think of things I did, of friends I knew and I wonder at life's changes.
I wish that things could remain the same, but I know they can not.*

21

CILLA AND CECIL
MY PROTECTOR

GLASS CHOICE:
Mermaid
Hair - wine/clear streaky and wine spectrum
Body - light wine mouthblown antique
Tail - wine seashell
Fins - pink baroque

Shark
Upper body - selected black baroque
Under body - Fremont milky purple antique
Lower fins - darker parts of milky purple antique

Water Stream
Clear waterglass

TECHNICAL DETAILS

Cecil's eye is a solder blob. Fins on Cilla could be extended with
tinned copperwire overlays for a spiky appearance (optional).
Hanging loop at hair join, edge beading. All features painted.

SERENDIPITY
CORAL CONTEMPLATION

GLASS CHOICE:
Mermaid
Hair - purple/blue/green streaky
Body - gold pink mouthblown antique
Tail - clear hammered
Fins - pink/clear streaky
Necklace - red glass bead

Pink glass fish (optional)

Coral table
Red/clear baroque
Red/clear bullseye

TECHNICAL DETAILS

Necklace tinned copperwire attached at neck. Glass
fish foiled at the appropriate spots then soldered at top
fin to hair, dorsal fin to hair and pectoral fin to
mermaids tail. Hanging loop tinned copperwire
soldered into hair join. Finish with edge beading.
Features painted with black enamel.

CIARA AND CALYPSO
LIFE IN A GOLDFISH BOWL

Life in a goldfish bowl my friend,
Is not all it's cracked up to be
We have to perform all day long
Whilst dreaming to be free.

CASSANDRA AND SEBASTION
SEALED WITH A LOVING KISS

We had a chance meeting in the sea one day.
Curious glances were exchanged and you edged
shyly closer with a twist and a twirl.
Before we knew it we began to play and we
frolicked on for hours and more.
Then something happened that made me tremble.
Warm and trusting, soft and gentle,
you sealed our friendship with a loving kiss!

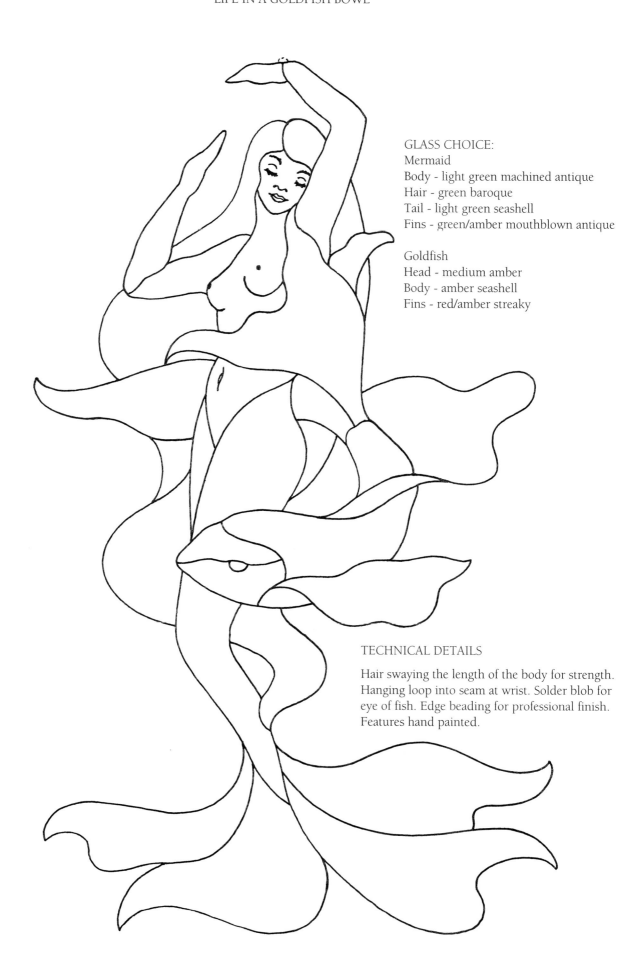

GLASS CHOICE:
Mermaid
Body - light green machined antique
Hair - green baroque
Tail - light green seashell
Fins - green/amber mouthblown antique

Goldfish
Head - medium amber
Body - amber seashell
Fins - red/amber streaky

TECHNICAL DETAILS

Hair swaying the length of the body for strength.
Hanging loop into seam at wrist. Solder blob for
eye of fish. Edge beading for professional finish.
Features hand painted.

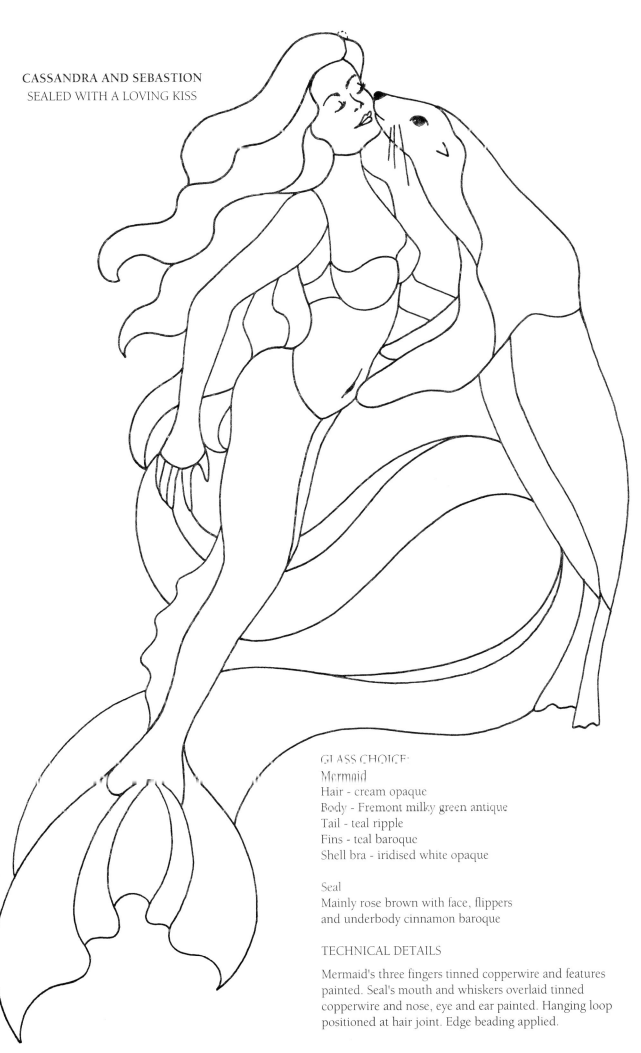

CASSANDRA AND SEBASTION
SEALED WITH A LOVING KISS

GLASS CHOICE:
Mermaid
Hair - cream opaque
Body - Fremont milky green antique
Tail - teal ripple
Fins - teal baroque
Shell bra - iridised white opaque

Seal
Mainly rose brown with face, flippers
and underbody cinnamon baroque

TECHNICAL DETAILS

Mermaid's three fingers tinned copperwire and features
painted. Seal's mouth and whiskers overlaid tinned
copperwire and nose, eye and ear painted. Hanging loop
positioned at hair joint. Edge beading applied.

MIRRIM AND COCKLE
OFF TO THE RACES

We won't win the race but we'll take time to enjoy the view.

PHALENE WITH SNAP AND PIPI
MY TRANQUIL CORAL GARDEN

A kaleidoscope of colour passes by my eyes
This is my living garden   bright and so alive.
My flowers are anemones and corals by the score,
Shining fish and seaweed beds are right outside my door.
Their movements are in time with the rhythms of the sea
As they sway back and forth in gentle harmony.
Miracles surround me, amaze and astound me and make it hard to leave
my tranquil coral garden,
Of such extraordinary beauty, that I can hardly breathe.

37

MIRRIM AND COCKLE
OFF TO THE RACES

GLASS CHOICE:
Mermaid
Hair - white/clear streaky
Cap - red/amber streaky
Body - Fremont milky green antique
Tail - cream wismach
Bra - cream wismach
Fins - white/clear baroque

Turtle
Head - brown ring mottle
Flippers - brown ring mottle
Shell - green/amber ring mottle

TECHNICAL DETAILS

Cap has solder blob decorations applied. Turtle's
mouth is overlaid tinned copperwire. Turtle's lead
is ball chain attached with solder to appropriate
points and left to hang free between them. Hanging
loop positioned at hair join and edge beading
applied. Features painted.

PHALENE WITH SNAP AND PIPI
MY TRANQUIL CORAL GARDEN

GLASS CHOICE:
Mermaid
Hair - blue/clear streaky
Body - cinnamon baroque
Tail - royal blue granite
Fins - red/amber streaky

Snap
Stripes - royal blue sahara
Stripes - golden yellow
Face - yellow antique
Side and dorsal fins - yellow waterglass
Upper and lower fins - dark blue waterglass

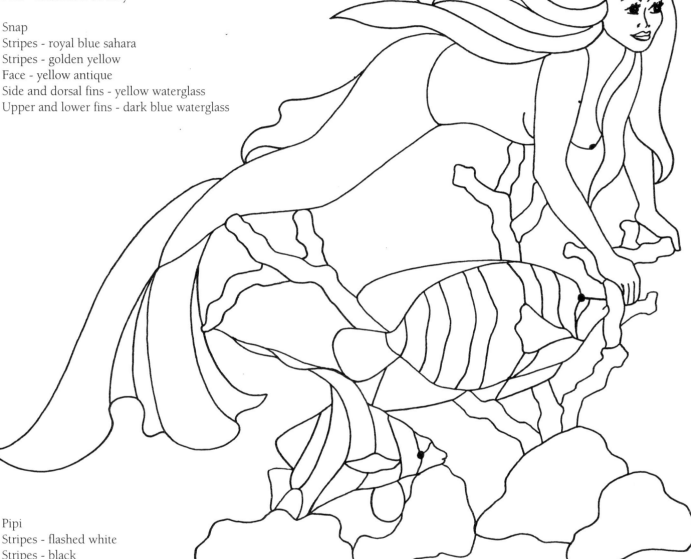

Pipi
Stripes - flashed white
Stripes - black
Fins - yellow opaque

Coral
Rocks - light and dark green seashell
Staghorn - cranberry ripple

Anemones (optional)
Beads - blue, red and green glass

Glass fish (optional)

TECHNICAL DETAILS

Fish eyes are applied solder blobs. Glass beads are threaded with fuse wire, bunched together and attached in between coral clumps with wires hidden in the back seams. Optional glass fish already has wire attached and is soldered into the appropriate position so as to appear to be swimming through the anemone. Fin from Pipi is wired for stability and attached to pink coral. Hanging loop is attached at third hair seam from face for proper balance. Edge beading for strength. Features painted.

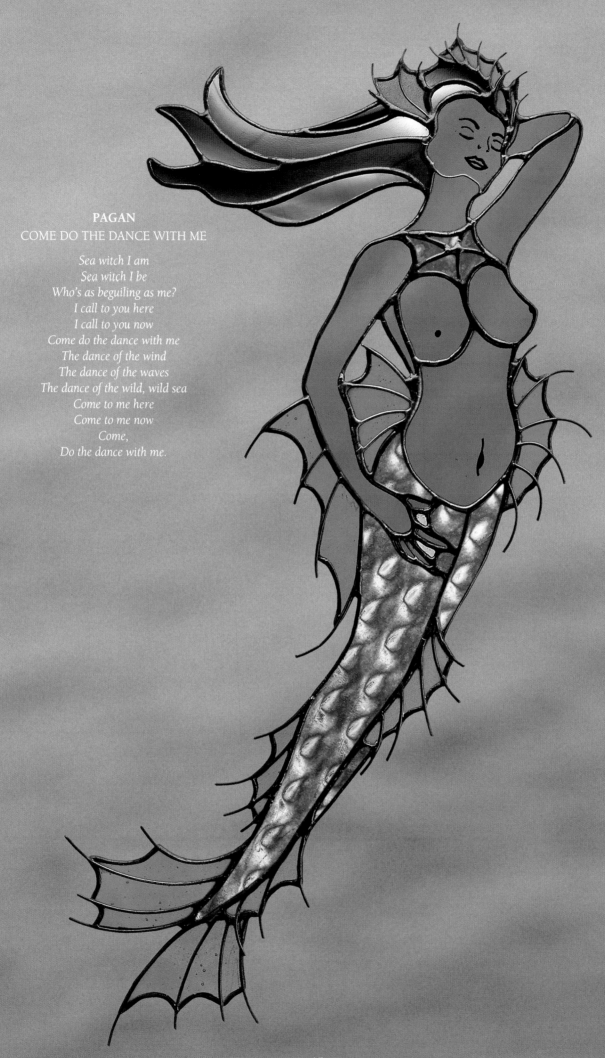

PAGAN
COME DO THE DANCE WITH ME

Sea witch I am
Sea witch I be
Who's as beguiling as me?
I call to you here
I call to you now
Come do the dance with me
The dance of the wind
The dance of the waves
The dance of the wild, wild sea
Come to me here
Come to me now
Come,
Do the dance with me.

FOAM AND BUBBLES
CAN YOU SEE THEM

Look, can you see them?
Aren't they beautiful?
They pass this way but once a year,
Then memory must serve, until they return.

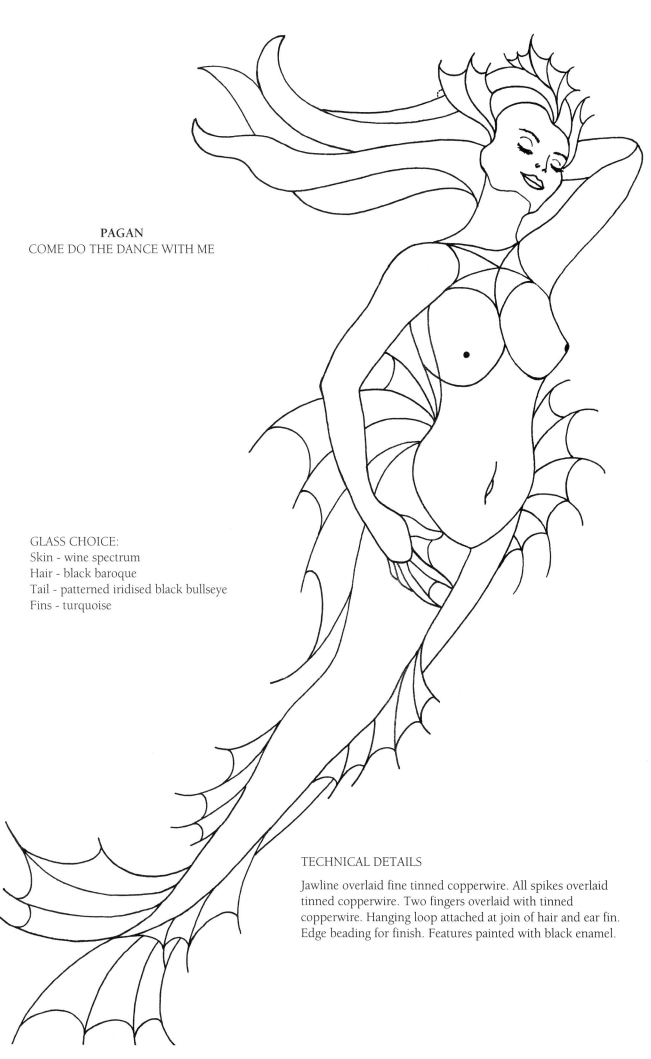

PAGAN
COME DO THE DANCE WITH ME

GLASS CHOICE:
Skin - wine spectrum
Hair - black baroque
Tail - patterned iridised black bullseye
Fins - turquoise

TECHNICAL DETAILS

Jawline overlaid fine tinned copperwire. All spikes overlaid tinned copperwire. Two fingers overlaid with tinned copperwire. Hanging loop attached at join of hair and ear fin. Edge beading for finish. Features painted with black enamel.

FOAM AND BUBBLES
CAN YOU SEE THEM?

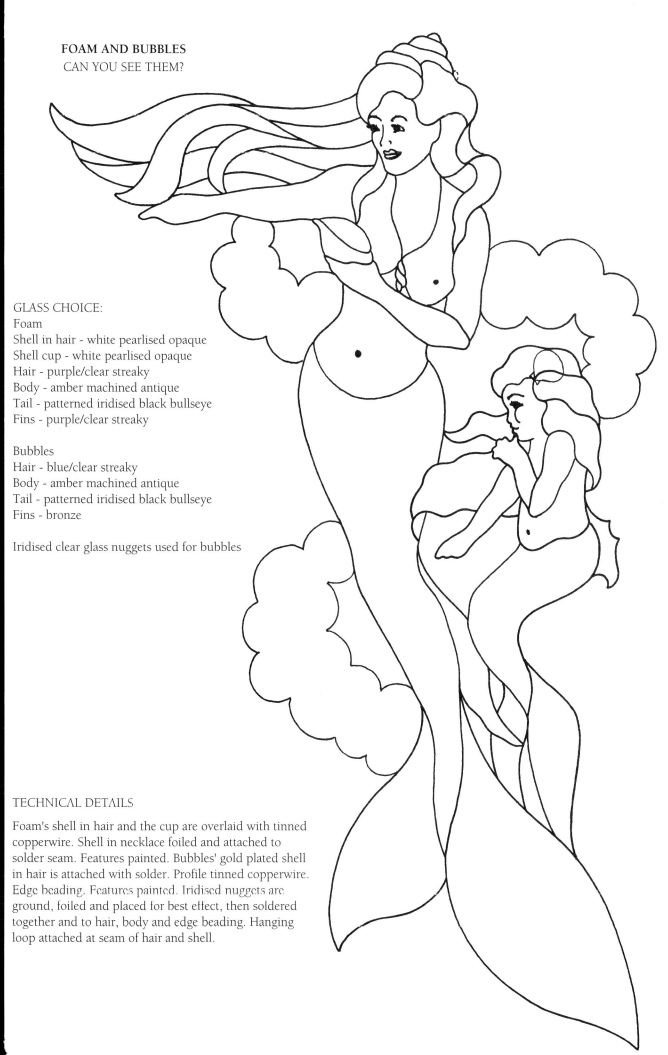

GLASS CHOICE:
Foam
Shell in hair - white pearlised opaque
Shell cup - white pearlised opaque
Hair - purple/clear streaky
Body - amber machined antique
Tail - patterned iridised black bullseye
Fins - purple/clear streaky

Bubbles
Hair - blue/clear streaky
Body - amber machined antique
Tail - patterned iridised black bullseye
Fins - bronze

Iridised clear glass nuggets used for bubbles

TECHNICAL DETAILS

Foam's shell in hair and the cup are overlaid with tinned copperwire. Shell in necklace foiled and attached to solder seam. Features painted. Bubbles' gold plated shell in hair is attached with solder. Profile tinned copperwire. Edge beading. Features painted. Iridised nuggets are ground, foiled and placed for best effect, then soldered together and to hair, body and edge beading. Hanging loop attached at seam of hair and shell.

CASCADIA AND BUECEPHEROUS
WILD WAVE RIDE

Proud spirit soaring
And so rarely seen
No sign where he's going
No sign where he's been
Wild water flow
Fierce wind blow
Send the white waves for me
Then he will come with elemental force
Out of the sea, to me
We'll share the thrill of the wild wave ride
This strange white horse
And me.

44

AVALON AND FLUTE
THE DOLPHIN SERENADE

My heart is filled with your music and I hear the words that you sing
Your song is of the wide blue seas and I will tell of the story you bring
I hear the swirls of happiness as the water caresses your form
As it touches your silken body and you remember the day you were born
I feel the sound that it makes as you breach and then you fall
I hear the silence of your run when you answer some urgent call
I hear it bubble and fizz and your excitement gradually grows
As you answer some need inside yourself that only you can know
Then I feel the wild explosive force as you leap for the nearest star
And you sing to me the contentment of being who you are.

GLASS CHOICE:
Mermaid
Hair - brown/amber streaky
Body - gold mouthblown antique
Tail - amber seashell
Fins - amber baroque

Horse
Head and body - flashed white
Hooves - amber
Mane - white opaque and blue/white opaque

Waves
Caps - white and cream opaque
Under - blue/clear baroque

TECHNICAL DETAILS

Horse's eye and nostrils are solder blobs.
Hanging loop positioned for balance, edge
beading for strength and features painted.

AVALON AND FLUTE
THE DOLPHIN SERENADE

GLASS CHOICE:
Mermaid
Hair - red/amber streaky
Body - light amber machined antique
Tail - orange
Fins - light orange
Seaweed - green ripple
Rock - brown streaky
Sea - blue/clear streaky

Bird
Flashed white
Underwing and small side of tail - white streaky

Air Stream
Clear seedy

Dolphin
Steel blue waterglass
Light blue mouthblown antique

TECHNICAL DETAILS

Face left clear of foil for effect, grind
very carefully using 6mm head. Bird's
beak is soldered copperwire. Dolphin's
eye is solder blob. Hanging loop is
tinned copperwire. Edge beading for
professional finish. Features painted
with black enamel.

*So this is where the otters dance
In this sea of waving kelp?
Oh? You say it's more than that.
It's where you come to whelp
It anchors you when you feed
And hides you from your foe
In fact, it's the cradle of your life
And without it you've nowhere to go.*

KIMI AND CONCH
SHY LITTLE FRIEND

Don't run away my shy little friend,
I've something to say to you.
But every time I get close, you scuttle away,
Or hide in your pretty shell.
You're no good in there, so come out if you dare
And you'll find you have friends who care.

LIANNA AND "CHOPPER"
A FROLIC WITH THE OTTER

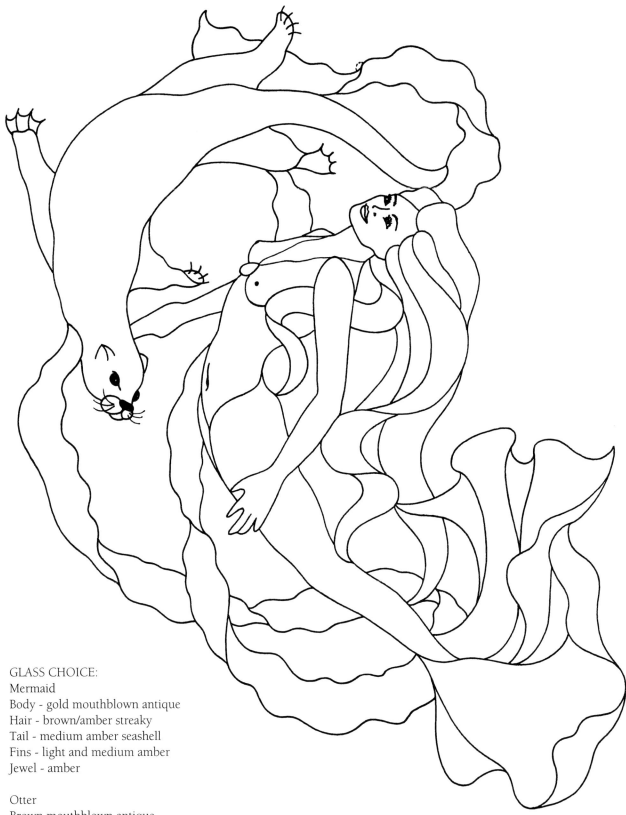

GLASS CHOICE:
Mermaid
Body - gold mouthblown antique
Hair - brown/amber streaky
Tail - medium amber seashell
Fins - light and medium amber
Jewel - amber

Otter
Brown mouthblown antique

TECHNICAL DETAILS

Claws and whiskers on otter are tinned copperwire attached with solder after edge beading. One eye is solder blob on the edge beading, other eye and ear painted. Mermaid's hand is foil cut to shape and soldered, for spaces between fingers. Hanging loop attached into seam in the seaweed above the otter's tail. Edge beading for strength. Features hand painted with black enamel paint.

KIMI AND CONCH
SHY LITTLE FRIEND

GLASS CHOICE:
Mermaid
Hair - rusty red/clear streaky
Body - pale amber seedy
Tail - red granite
Fins - red baroque

Crab
Shell - flashed white
Claws - flashed red on clear bariole

Extras
Brain coral - green seashell
Sea grass - green waterglass, green spectrum
Rock - brown/white streaky wismach

Anemone (optional)
Beads - amber glass

TECHNICAL DETAILS

Anemone made of glass beads threaded with fuse wire, bunched
together and soldered between the coral and rock. The crab's eye
stalks are tinned heavy guage copperwire with solder blobs on the
ends, soldered into position. Feelers are also tinned copperwire. The
hanging loop is positioned at the join of the hair and shoulder for
balance. Edge beading for strength. Features painted.

SERENITY AND SPLASH
MY COMPANION

Together we've travelled for many a year from sea to shining sea.
And of all the wonders we have seen,
the scrapes that we've been through.
Nothing has meant as much to me as the friendship I've shared with you.

DUSK, DAWN AND FUTURE
UNTIL TOMORROW

We've never seen your like before, or know from whence you come
You speak to us of wondrous places and deeds that you have done.
Now you have to go, and that leaves us filled with sorrow,
But you made a promise and happily we say,
Goodbye until tomorrow.

GLASS CHOICE:
Mermaid
Hair - blue/green/purple streaky
Body - light wine mouthblown antique
Tail - iridised cranberry bullseye
Fins - multi-coloured bullseye ripple (special)

Dolphin
Upper body - grey
Flukes - grey
Lower body - blue grey

TECHNICAL DETAILS

Dolphin's eye is solder blob. Hanging loop soldered into hair
seam at side of face. Edge beading for durability and finish.
Features painted with black enamel.

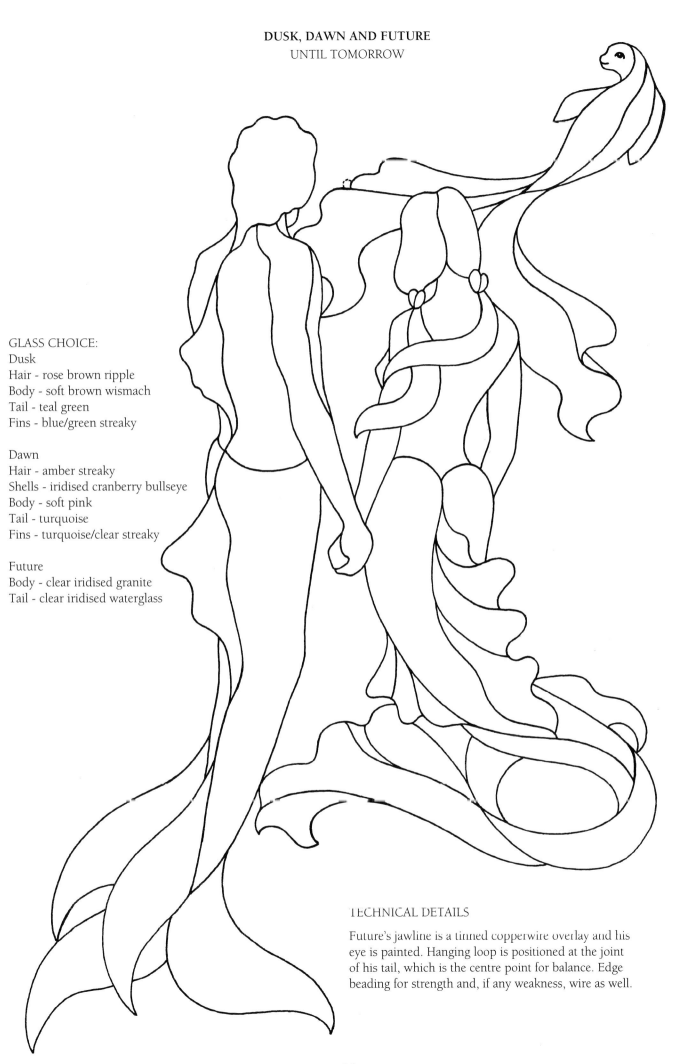

GLASS CHOICE:
Dusk
Hair - rose brown ripple
Body - soft brown wismach
Tail - teal green
Fins - blue/green streaky

Dawn
Hair - amber streaky
Shells - iridised cranberry bullseye
Body - soft pink
Tail - turquoise
Fins - turquoise/clear streaky

Future
Body - clear iridised granite
Tail - clear iridised waterglass

TECHNICAL DETAILS

Future's jawline is a tinned copperwire overlay and his
eye is painted. Hanging loop is positioned at the joint
of his tail, which is the centre point for balance. Edge
beading for strength and, if any weakness, wire as well.

ETCETERA

All mermaids are enlarged to twice the size shown in this book for ease of construction.

These patterns can be adapted for window panels as illustrated by pages (12 and 32), (13 and 33), (20 and 28) and (29 and 52).

Let YOUR imagination inspire YOUR glass choice.

Make good use of colour, grain of glass, flow of glass and mixture of glass types and textures. In effect, learn how to paint with your glass. EXPERIMENT! Sometimes, glass used in unexpected ways can add that extra sparkle or lift to your piece. For instance, a monochrome theme can be made startling with the effective use of one brightly opposing colour!

Always use good quality solder and liquid flux (3mm 60/40 solid core wire solder is the best). I use an 80watt soldering iron with an iron clad chisel tip. These tips never need filing and can be retinned if necessary, using a block of solid sal ammoniac. Keep your tip clean during the soldering process by frequently running it through a sponge dampened with water. This impedes the build up of impurities on your solder seam, which can hinder the cleaning and patina process.

Edge beading is used to give your piece extra strength and durability and to produce a finished, professional look. This is achieved by holding your piece on the edge. Using the flat of your tip to apply solder, hold still a few seconds until solder has solidified, then tilt your piece and repeat until you have built up a nice edge all around. Keep the spot you are working on level until solder sets - if you are slightly tilted in either direction, the solder will roll, resulting in an uneven bead. To prevent accidents always support your piece to one side of the area you are beading, never underneath, and wear protective gloves.

To apply solder blobs to the end of tinned wire, hold one end with pliers and pick up a small amount of solder on your iron. Place the tip in contact with the fluxed wire and the solder will run down the wire and form a ball on the end. At this point, remove the iron from the wire and with the heat source removed, the solder blob will solidify. If all steps are followed carefully and with slow, steady movements, you will soon have this procedure under control.

Always clean and patina your piece immediately you have finished soldering to avoid oxidization of seams. Oxidization will impede successful patination.